MW00956080

NOTEBOOK

designed to be used with

Cracking Chinese Characters: HSK 1, 2, 3, 4

LEARN CHINESE SMARTER

Copyright © 2017 HSK Academy

All rights reserved.

No part of this book may be used or reproduced in any manner whatsoever without written permission.

HSK Academy is not endorsed by any institution or company regarding the official HSK tests and cannot guarantee the accuracy or completeness of any published content on that regard, thus cannot be held responsible for any direct or indirect damages resulting from any use of it.

Cover picture: Emperor Kangxi, second emperor of the Qing Dynasty (The Palace Museum, Beijing)

For more information and contact: www.hsk.academy

ISBN-10: 1979045739
ISBN-13: 978-1979045735

FOREWORD

This notebook is designed to be used with **Cracking Chinese Characters: HSK 1, 2, 3, 4**: 1,000+ frequent characters deciphered to learn and remember them faster.

As such, this notebook will help you, learner of Chinese or HSK candidate, to focus on the 1,064 most common Chinese characters, the same as those required to pass the HSK tests of levels 1 to 4. It offers the same list of characters, sorted in alphabetic order (based on pinyin) with simplified Chinese, HSK level, pinyin, main meaning, and a wide blank space available for your own notes, drawings or whatever you want to add that helps you learn and remember. Most of the information you need to remember a character is available in **Cracking Chinese Characters: HSK 1, 2, 3, 4**, which gives you the list of buiding blocks to decipher characters, with phonetic hints. Take advantage of it to build your own way to remember characters, for instance through stories using mnemonic creatures for each character, as explained in the book, and keep track of them in this notebook. Regularity and frequent refreshing are other key success factors. Just flip the pages of this notebook to monitor your progress and remember what you have learnt so far. When it will be full: — Congratulations — you will have just done it.

We hope it will help you achieve your goal of learning Chinese smarter and succeed with the HSK tests faster.

Available on Amazon. Visit **bit.ly/HSKbooks** for more information

© HSK Academy

啊 hsk 3

a

modal particle showing affirmation, approval, or consent

阿 hsk 3

ā

prefix to indicate familiarity

矮 hsk 3

ǎi

short (in length)

爱 hsk 1

ài

to love

安 hsk 3

ān

secure, calm

按 hsk 4

àn

to press, according to

案 hsk 4

àn

(legal) case, record

傲 hsk 4

ào

proud

吧 hsk 2

ba

modal particle indicating suggestion or surmise

八 hsk 1

bā

eight

把 hsk 3
bǎ
to hold

爸 hsk 1
bà
father

白 hsk 2
bái
white

百 hsk 2
bǎi
hundred

败 hsk 4
bài
to defeat

拜 hsk 4
bài
to pay respect

班 hsk 2
bān
team

般 hsk 3
bān
sort, kind

搬 hsk 3
bān
to move (something or to relocate oneself)

板 hsk 3
bǎn
board

办 hsk 3
bàn
to do

半 hsk 3
bàn
half

扮 hsk 4
bàn
to disguise oneself as

帮 hsk 2
bāng
to help

棒 hsk 4
bàng
excellent, stick

包 hsk 3
bāo
to cover

饱 hsk 3
bǎo
to eat till full

保 hsk 4
bǎo
to defend

报 hsk 2
bào
to announce

抱 hsk 4
bào
to hold

杯 hsk 1
bēi
cup

北 hsk 1
běi
north

备 hsk 2
bèi
to prepare

倍 hsk 4
bèi
times (multiplier), (two, three) fold

被 hsk 3
bèi
quilt

本 hsk 1
běn
roots or stems of plants

笨 hsk 4
bèn
stupid

鼻 hsk 3
bí
nose

比 hsk 2
bǐ
to associate with

笔 hsk 2
bǐ
pen

必 hsk 3
bì
certainly, must

毕 hsk 4
bì
finish, complete

边 hsk 2
biān
side

变 hsk 3
biàn
to change

便 hsk 2
biàn
ordinary

遍 hsk 4
biàn
everywhere

标 hsk 4
biāo
sign, to mark

表 hsk 2
biǎo
surface, external, form, list

别 hsk 2
bié
do not

宾 hsk 2
bīn
visitor

冰 hsk 3

bīng

ice

饼 hsk 4

bǐng

round flat cake

并 hsk 4

bìng

to combine

病 hsk 2

bìng

illness

播 hsk 4

bō

to sow, to spread

博 hsk 4

bó

rich, erudit, to win, to gamble

膊 hsk 4

bó

shoulder

不 hsk 1

bù

(negative prefix)

步 hsk 2

bù

a step

部 hsk 4

bù

department, section

擦 hsk 4
cā
to wipe

猜 hsk 4
cāi
to guess

才 hsk 3
cái
ability, talent; late, indicating just happened

材 hsk 4
cái
material

彩 hsk 4
cǎi
(bright) color

菜 hsk 1
cài
dish (type of food)

参 hsk 3
cān
to take part in

餐 hsk 4
cān
meal

草 hsk 3
cǎo
grass

厕 hsk 4
cè
restroom, lavatory

层 hsk 3
céng
layer

查 hsk 3
chá
to research

茶 hsk 1
chá
tea

察 hsk 4
chá
to examine

差 hsk 3
chā / chà / chāi
different / wrong / dispatch

长 hsk 2
cháng / zhǎng
long, length / to grow, elder

尝 hsk 4
cháng
to taste

常 hsk 2
cháng
always

场 hsk 2
chǎng
large place used for a particular purpose

唱 hsk 2
chàng
to sing

超 hsk 3

chāo

to surpass

车 hsk 1

chē

car

衬 hsk 3

chèn

(of garments) against the skin

成 hsk 3

chéng

to accomplish, grow, become

诚 hsk 4

chéng

honest

城 hsk 3

chéng

city walls, town

乘 hsk 4

chéng

to ride

程 hsk 4

chéng

rule, procedure

吃 hsk 1

chī

to eat

迟 hsk 3

chí

late

持 hsk 4 **chí** to hold	抽 hsk 4 **chōu** to draw out
出 hsk 1 **chū** to go out	除 hsk 3 **chú** to get rid of
厨 hsk 4 **chú** kitchen	础 hsk 4 **chǔ** foundation
楚 hsk 3 **chǔ** distinct	处 hsk 4 **chù** place
穿 hsk 2 **chuān** to wear, to pierce	传 hsk 4 **chuán** to pass on

船 hsk 3 **chuán** boat	窗 hsk 4 **chuāng** window
床 hsk 2 **chuáng** bed	春 hsk 3 **chūn** spring (season), youth
词 hsk 3 **cí** word	此 hsk 4 **cǐ** this, these
次 hsk 2 **cì** next in sequence	聪 hsk 3 **cōng** clever
从 hsk 2 **cóng** from	粗 hsk 4 **cū** distant

存 hsk 4

cún

to store, deposit, exist

错 hsk 2

cuò

mistake

答 hsk 3

dá

reply

打 hsk 1

dǎ

to beat, to hit, to make, to play (a game)

大 hsk 1

dà / dài

big

带 hsk 3

dài

belt, to carry

袋 hsk 4

dài

bag, pocket

戴 hsk 4

dài

to put on, wear

单 hsk 3

dān

list, form

担 hsk 3

dān

to undertake

但 hsk 2
dàn
but

蛋 hsk 2
dàn
egg

当 hsk 3
dāng / dàng
to be equal, act as; when / proper, appropriate

刀 hsk 4
dāo
knife

导 hsk 4
dǎo
to transmit

到 hsk 2
dào
to (a place)

倒 hsk 4
dào
to place upside down

道 hsk 2
dào
road, direction, principle

地 hsk 3
de / dì
#NAME?

的 hsk 1
de / dì
of, ~'s (possessive part.) / target

得 hsk 2

de / dé

(struct. part.) indicating effect, degree, possibility / to obtain

灯 hsk 3

dēng

lamp

登 hsk 4

dēng

to step on

等 hsk 2

děng

to wait, rank

低 hsk 4

dī

low

底 hsk 4

dǐ

background, bottom, end (of the month, year…)

弟 hsk 2

dì

younger brother

第 hsk 2

dì

(prefix indicating ordinal number, e.g. first, number two etc)

典 hsk 3

diǎn

standard work of scholarship

点 hsk 1

diǎn

point, dot, drop, o'clock

电 hsk 1
diàn
electric

店 hsk 1
diàn
shop

调 hsk 3
diào / tiáo
to transfer, investigate / to harmonize, regulate

掉 hsk 4
diào
to fall

定 hsk 3
dìng
to set, to fix, calm, stable

丢 hsk 4
diū
to lose

东 hsk 1
dōng
east

冬 hsk 3
dōng
winter

懂 hsk 2
dǒng
to understand

动 hsk 2
dòng
(of sth) to move

都 hsk 1 **dōu / dū** all / capital	读 hsk 1 **dú** to read
堵 hsk 4 **dǔ** to stop up	肚 hsk 4 **dù** stomach
度 hsk 4 **dù** measure	短 hsk 3 **duǎn** short
段 hsk 3 **duàn** paragraph	断 hsk 4 **duàn** to break
锻 hsk 3 **duàn** to forge	队 hsk 4 **duì** team, group

对 hsk 1
duì
correct, opposite

多 hsk 1
duō
many

朵 hsk 3
duǒ
earlobe

饿 hsk 3
è
to be hungry

儿 hsk 1
er
child; son; (suffix to express smallness)

而 hsk 3
ér
and, but (not), if

尔 hsk 4
ěr
thus

耳 hsk 3
ěr
ear

二 hsk 1
èr
two

发 hsk 3
fā
to send out

法 hsk 3
fǎ
law

翻 hsk 4
fān
to turn over, to decode

烦 hsk 4
fán
to feel vexed

反 hsk 4
fǎn
contrary

饭 hsk 1
fàn
food

方 hsk 3
fāng
square

房 hsk 2
fáng
house

放 hsk 3
fàng
to release

飞 hsk 1
fēi
to fly

非 hsk 2
fēi
to not be

啡 hsk 2

fēi

phonetic component for (co)ffee

肥 hsk 4

féi

fat

费 hsk 4

fèi

to cost

分 hsk 1

fēn

to divide

份 hsk 4

fèn

part; classifier for portion or copy of a paper

奋 hsk 4

fèn

to exert oneself

丰 hsk 4

fēng

luxuriant

风 hsk 3

fēng

wind

封 hsk 4

fēng

to confer

否 hsk 4

fǒu

to negate

夫 hsk 2

fū

husband, man, manual worker

肤 hsk 4

fū

skin

服 hsk 1

fú

clothes

符 hsk 4

fú

sign, symbol, to correspond to

福 hsk 4

fú

happiness, luck

父 hsk 4

fù

father

付 hsk 4

fù

to pay

负 hsk 4

fù

to bear

附 hsk 3

fù

to be close to, to add

复 hsk 3

fù

to repeat, complex (not simple)

傅 hsk 4
fù
instructor

富 hsk 4
fù
rich

该 hsk 3
gāi
should

改 hsk 4
gǎi
to change

概 hsk 4
gài
in general

赶 hsk 4
gǎn
to overtake

敢 hsk 4
gǎn
to dare

感 hsk 3
gǎn
to feel

干 hsk 3
gān / gàn
dry, empty / to do, to work as, to oppose

刚 hsk 3
gāng
hard, just, exactly

钢 hsk 4

gāng

steel

高 hsk 1

gāo

high

膏 hsk 4

gāo

ointment, paste

糕 hsk 3

gāo

cake

告 hsk 2

gào

to say

哥 hsk 2

gē

elder brother

胳 hsk 4

gē

armpit

歌 hsk 2

gē

song

格 hsk 4

gé

frame, square, pattern

个 hsk 1

gè

general classifier for people or objects

各 hsk 4 **gè** each	给 hsk 2 **gěi** for the benefit of
根 hsk 3 **gēn** root, source, basis	跟 hsk 3 **gēn** to go with, compared with, heel
更 hsk 3 **gèng** even more	工 hsk 1 **gōng** work
公 hsk 2 **gōng** public	功 hsk 4 **gōng** achievement, result
供 hsk 4 **gōng** to provide	共 hsk 2 **gòng** common

狗 hsk 1
gǒu
dog

购 hsk 4
gòu
to buy

够 hsk 4
gòu
enough, sufficient

估 hsk 4
gū / gù
to estimate / old (of things)

鼓 hsk 4
gǔ
drum, to rouse

故 hsk 3
gù
ancient

顾 hsk 3
gù
to look after

瓜 hsk 2
guā
melon

刮 hsk 3
guā
to scrape

挂 hsk 4
guà
to hang or suspend (from a hook etc)

怪 hsk 3 **guài** bewildering, odd	关 hsk 1 **guān** to close
观 hsk 4 **guān** to look at	馆 hsk 2 **guǎn** building
管 hsk 4 **guǎn** to take care (of)	惯 hsk 3 **guàn** accustomed to
光 hsk 4 **guāng** light	广 hsk 4 **guǎng** wide
逛 hsk 4 **guàng** to stroll	规 hsk 4 **guī** rule, regulation

贵 hsk 2

guì

expensive

国 hsk 1

guó

country

果 hsk 1

guǒ

fruit

过 hsk 2

guò

to cross, to get along, to pass (time)

还 hsk 2

hái / huán

still, in progress / to pay back, return

孩 hsk 2

hái

child

海 hsk 4

hǎi

ocean

害 hsk 3

hài

to do harm to

寒 hsk 4

hán

chilly

汉 hsk 1

hàn

Chinese (language)

汗 hsk 4
hàn
perspiration

行 hsk 3
háng / xíng
professionnal / to travel

航 hsk 4
háng
boat

好 hsk 1
hǎo / hào
good / to be fond of

号 hsk 1
hào
ordinal number

喝 hsk 1
hē
to drink

合 hsk 4
hé
to join, to suit, to close, to shut

何 hsk 4
hé
who, whom, what, which

和 hsk 1
hé
and

河 hsk 3
hé
river

盒 hsk 4 **hé** small box	贺 hsk 4 **hè** to congratulate
黑 hsk 2 **hēi** black	很 hsk 1 **hěn** very
红 hsk 2 **hóng** red	后 hsk 1 **hòu** behind, later
厚 hsk 4 **hòu** thick	候 hsk 1 **hòu** to wait
乎 hsk 3 **hū** part. (expressing question or astonishment), in, at, from	呼 hsk 4 **hū** to breathe out, to shout, to call

虎 hsk 4

hǔ

tiger

互 hsk 4

hù

mutual

户 hsk 4

hù

door, household

护 hsk 3

hù

to protect

花 hsk 3

huā

flower, to spend

化 hsk 3

huà

to make into

划 hsk 4

huà

to delimit

画 hsk 3

huà

to draw

话 hsk 1

huà

dialect

怀 hsk 4

huái

to conceive

坏 hsk 3
huài
bad

欢 hsk 1
huān
joyous

环 hsk 3
huán
ring

换 hsk 3
huàn
to exchange

黄 hsk 3
huáng
yellow

回 hsk 1
huí
to return

悔 hsk 4
huǐ
to regret

会 hsk 1
huì
to understand, have knowledge of, be able to, be good at, get together

婚 hsk 3
hūn
to marry

活 hsk 4
huó
to live

火 hsk 2

huǒ

fire

伙 hsk 4

huǒ

partner, mate

或 hsk 3

huò

maybe

货 hsk 4

huò

goods, money, commodities

获 hsk 4

huò

to reap

圾 hsk 4

jī

rubbish

机 hsk 1

jī

machine

鸡 hsk 2

jī

chicken

积 hsk 4

jī

to amass

基 hsk 4

jī

base

激 hsk 4
jī
to arouse

及 hsk 4
jí
and

级 hsk 3
jí
level

即 hsk 4
jí
to approach, prompted by the occasion, now

极 hsk 3
jí
extremely

急 hsk 3
jí
urgent

籍 hsk 4
jí
record, registry, membership

几 hsk 1
jǐ / jī
how many / small table

己 hsk 3
jǐ
oneself

计 hsk 4
jì
to calculate

记 hsk 3

jì

to record

纪 hsk 4

jì

era, period

技 hsk 4

jì

skill

际 hsk 4

jì

border

季 hsk 3

jì

season

既 hsk 4

jì

adv. already; conj. since, now that

济 hsk 4

jì

to be of help, to cross a river

继 hsk 4

jì

to continue

绩 hsk 3

jī

merit, accomplishment, grade

寄 hsk 4

jì

to send, to entrust

加 hsk 3
jiā
to add

家 hsk 1
jiā
home

假 hsk 3
jiǎ / jià
false / vacation

价 hsk 4
jià
price

坚 hsk 4
jiān
strong

间 hsk 2
jiān
between, room

减 hsk 4
jiǎn
to lower

检 hsk 3
jiǎn
to check

简 hsk 3
jiǎn
simple

见 hsk 1
jiàn
to see

件 hsk 2
jiàn
item

建 hsk 4
jiàn
to establish

健 hsk 3
jiàn
to invigorate

键 hsk 4
jiàn
key (on a piano or computer keyboard)

江 hsk 4
jiāng
river

将 hsk 4
jiāng
will, shall

讲 hsk 3
jiǎng
to speak, tell

奖 hsk 4
jiǎng
prize

降 hsk 4
jiàng
to come down

交 hsk 4
jiāo
to hand over

郊 hsk 4
jiāo
suburbs

骄 hsk 4
jiāo
haughty

蕉 hsk 3
jiāo
banana

角 hsk 3
jiǎo / jué
angle, corner / role

饺 hsk 4
jiǎo
dumplings with meat filling

脚 hsk 3
jiǎo
foot

叫 hsk 1
jiào
to be called

觉 hsk 1
jiào / jué
a nap / to feel

较 hsk 3
jiào
comparatively

教 hsk 2
jiào
to teach, to instruct

接 hsk 3
jiē
to receive

街 hsk 3
jiē
street

节 hsk 3
jié
festival

结 hsk 3
jié
knot, bond

姐 hsk 1
jiě
older sister

解 hsk 3
jiě
to divide

介 hsk 2
jiè
to introduce

界 hsk 3
jiè
boundary

借 hsk 3
jiè
to lend

巾 hsk 4
jīn
towel

今 hsk 1

jīn

today

斤 hsk 3

jīn

weight equal to 0.5 kg

金 hsk 4

jīn

gold

仅 hsk 4

jǐn

barely

尽 hsk 4

jǐn / jìn

to the greatest extent / to use up

紧 hsk 4

jǐn

tight

近 hsk 2

jìn

near

进 hsk 2

jìn

to enter, to advance

禁 hsk 4

jìn

to prohibit

京 hsk 1

jīng

capital city of a country, abbr. for 北京 Běijīng

经 hsk 2

jīng

to pass through

惊 hsk 4

jīng

to startle, to be scared

睛 hsk 2

jīng

eyeball

精 hsk 4

jīng

essence, vitality, energy

景 hsk 4

jǐng

bright

警 hsk 4

jǐng

to alert

净 hsk 3

jìng

clean

竞 hsk 4

jìng

to compete

竟 hsk 4

jìng

finish, unexpectedly

境 hsk 3

jìng

border

静 hsk 3
jìng
calm

镜 hsk 4
jìng
mirror

究 hsk 4
jiū
to investigate, actually

九 hsk 1
jiǔ
nine

久 hsk 3
jiǔ
(long) time

酒 hsk 3
jiǔ
alcoholic beverage

旧 hsk 3
jiù
old (by opposition to new)

就 hsk 2
jiù
just (emphasis), at once

居 hsk 3
jū
to reside

局 hsk 4
jú
office

举 hsk 4

jǔ

to lift

句 hsk 3

jù

sentence

拒 hsk 4

jù

to resist

具 hsk 4

jù

tool

剧 hsk 4

jù

drama

据 hsk 3

jù

according to

距 hsk 4

jù

at a distance of

聚 hsk 4

jù

to congregate

决 hsk 3

jué

to decide

绝 hsk 4

jué

to cut short

咖 hsk 2

kā

phonetic component for co(ffee)

卡 hsk 3

kǎ

to stop

开 hsk 1

kāi

to open, start

看 hsk 1

kàn

to look at

康 hsk 3

kāng

healthy

考 hsk 2

kǎo

to check

烤 hsk 4

kǎo

to roast

科 hsk 4

kē

branch of study

棵 hsk 4

kē

classifier for trees, cabbages, plants etc

咳 hsk 4

ké / hāi

cough / interj. sound of sighing (to express sadness, regret, surprise)

可 hsk 2	渴 hsk 3
kě	**kě**
can, may	thirsty
克 hsk 4	刻 hsk 3
kè	**kè**
to be able to	quarter (hour)
客 hsk 1	课 hsk 2
kè	**kè**
visitor	subject
肯 hsk 4	空 hsk 3
kěn	**kōng**
to agree	empty
恐 hsk 4	口 hsk 3
kǒng	**kǒu**
afraid	mouth

哭 hsk 3
kū
to cry

苦 hsk 4
kǔ
bitter

裤 hsk 3
kù
underpants

块 hsk 1
kuài
unit of currency, chunk, piece

快 hsk 2
kuài
rapid

筷 hsk 3
kuài
chopstick

款 hsk 4
kuǎn
item, paragraph, section, funds

况 hsk 4
kuàng
moreover

矿 hsk 4
kuàng
mineral deposit, ore

困 hsk 4
kùn
to trap

垃 hsk 4
lā
garbage

拉 hsk 4
lā
to pull

辣 hsk 4
là
hot (spicy)

来 hsk 1
lái
to come

蓝 hsk 3
lán
blue

篮 hsk 2
lán
basket

懒 hsk 4
lǎn
lazy

浪 hsk 4
làng
wave

老 hsk 1
lǎo
old (of people)

了 hsk 1
le / liǎo
(completed action marker) / to finish

乐 hsk 2 **lè / yuè** happy / music	累 hsk 2 **lèi** tired
冷 hsk 1 **lěng** cold	离 hsk 2 **lí** to leave
礼 hsk 3 **lǐ** gift, rite, courtesy	李 hsk 3 **lǐ** plum
里 hsk 1 **lǐ** inside	理 hsk 3 **lǐ** to manage, to pay attention to, intrinsic order
力 hsk 3 **lì** power	历 hsk 3 **lì** to pass through

厉 hsk 4 **lì** strict	丽 hsk 4 **lì** beautiful
利 hsk 4 **lì** advantage, profit, sharp	励 hsk 4 **lì** to encourage
例 hsk 4 **lì** example	俩 hsk 4 **liǎ** both, some
连 hsk 4 **lián** to link	怜 hsk 4 **lián** to pity
联 hsk 4 **lián** to ally	脸 hsk 3 **liǎn** face

练 hsk 3
liàn
to practice

炼 hsk 3
liàn
to refine

凉 hsk 4
liáng
cool, cold

两 hsk 2
liǎng
two (quantity)

亮 hsk 1
liàng
clear

谅 hsk 4
liàng
to forgive

辆 hsk 3
liàng
classifier for vehicles

量 hsk 4
liàng / liáng
quantity / to measure

聊 hsk 3
liáo
to chat

料 hsk 3
liào
material, stuff, to anticipate

列 hsk 4
liè
to arrange

邻 hsk 3
lín
neighbor

林 hsk 4
lín
woods

零 hsk 2
líng
zero

龄 hsk 4
líng
length of experience, membership etc

另 hsk 4
lìng
other, separate

流 hsk 4
liú
to flow

留 hsk 3
liú
to stay, to remain

六 hsk 1
liù
six

楼 hsk 3
lóu
floor

旅 hsk 2 **lǚ** trip	路 hsk 2 **lù** road
律 hsk 4 **lǜ** law	虑 hsk 4 **lǜ** to think over
绿 hsk 3 **lǜ** green	乱 hsk 4 **luàn** in confusion or disorder
论 hsk 4 **lùn** opinion	落 hsk 4 **luò** to fall or drop
吗 hsk 1 **ma** (question tag)	妈 hsk 1 **mā** mom

麻 hsk 4

má

feeling pins and needles, numb, generic name for hemp, flax etc

马 hsk 3

mǎ

horse

码 hsk 4

mǎ

weight

买 hsk 1

mǎi

to buy

卖 hsk 2

mài

to sell

满 hsk 3

mǎn

to fill

慢 hsk 2

màn

slow

漫 hsk 4

màn

free, unrestrained

忙 hsk 2

máng

busy

猫 hsk 1

māo

cat

毛 hsk 4
máo
hair, feather

冒 hsk 3
mào
to emit

帽 hsk 3
mào
hat

貌 hsk 4
mào
appearance

么 hsk 1
me
used to form interrogative 什么

没 hsk 1
méi
(negative prefix for verbs)

每 hsk 2
měi
each

美 hsk 4
měi
beautiful, abbr. for the Americas

妹 hsk 2
mèi
younger sister

们 hsk 1
men
plural marker for pronouns

门 hsk 2
mén
gate

梦 hsk 4
mèng
dream

迷 hsk 4
mí
to bewilder

米 hsk 1
mǐ
rice

密 hsk 4
mì
secret

免 hsk 4
miǎn
to excuse somebody, to exempt

面 hsk 1
miàn
face

秒 hsk 4
miǎo
second (of time)

民 hsk 4
mín
the people

名 hsk 1
míng
name

明 hsk 1
míng
bright

命 hsk 4
mìng
life

末 hsk 3
mò
end

默 hsk 4
mò
silent

母 hsk 4
mǔ
mother

目 hsk 3
mù
eye

慕 hsk 4
mù
to admire

拿 hsk 3
ná
to hold

哪 hsk 1
nǎ
how

那 hsk 1
nà
that

奶 hsk 2
nǎi
milk, breast

耐 hsk 4
nài
capable of enduring

男 hsk 2
nán
male

南 hsk 3
nán
south

难 hsk 3
nán
difficult

恼 hsk 4
nǎo
to get angry

脑 hsk 1
nǎo
brain

闹 hsk 4
nào
noisy

呢 hsk 1
ne
(marker of declarative, interrogative or alternative statements)

内 hsk 4
nèi
inside

能 hsk 1
néng
can

你 hsk 1
nǐ
you (informal)

年 hsk 1
nián
year

鸟 hsk 3
niǎo
bird

您 hsk 2
nín
you (courteous)

牛 hsk 2
niú
ox

弄 hsk 4
nòng
to do

努 hsk 3
nǔ
to exert

女 hsk 1
nǚ
female

暖 hsk 4
nuǎn
warm

偶 hsk 4

ǒu

accidental, idol

爬 hsk 3

pá

to crawl

怕 hsk 3

pà

to be afraid

排 hsk 4

pái

to arrange, put in order, a row

牌 hsk 4

pái

(playing) card, brand

盘 hsk 3

pán

plate

判 hsk 4

pàn

to judge

乓 hsk 4

pāng

(onom.) pang

旁 hsk 2

páng

beside

胖 hsk 3

pàng

fat

跑 hsk 2
pǎo
to run

陪 hsk 4
péi
to accompany

朋 hsk 1
péng
friend

批 hsk 4
pī
to ascertain

皮 hsk 3
pí
leather

啤 hsk 3
pí
beer

脾 hsk 4
pí
spleen

篇 hsk 4
piān
sheet

片 hsk 3
piàn
thin piece, slice

骗 hsk 4
piàn
to cheat

票 hsk 2

piào

ticket

漂 hsk 1

piào

elegant

聘 hsk 4

pìn

to engage (someone)

乒 hsk 4

pīng

(onom.) ping

平 hsk 3

píng

flat, level, to draw (score)

评 hsk 4

píng

to discuss

苹 hsk 1

píng

apple

瓶 hsk 3

píng

bottle

泼 hsk 4

pō

to splash

破 hsk 4

pò

broken

葡 hsk 4

pú

grape, abbr. for Portugal

普 hsk 4

pǔ

general

七 hsk 1

qī

seven

妻 hsk 2

qī

wife

戚 hsk 4

qī

relative (family)

期 hsk 1

qī

a period of time

其 hsk 3

qí

his

奇 hsk 3

qí

strange

骑 hsk 3

qí

to ride (an animal or a bike)

起 hsk 1

qǐ

to rise

气 hsk 1
qì
gas

弃 hsk 4
qì
to abandon

汽 hsk 2
qì
steam

千 hsk 2
qiān
thousand

铅 hsk 2
qiān
lead (chemistry)

签 hsk 4
qiān
to sign one's name

前 hsk 1
qián
ahead

钱 hsk 1
qián
coin

歉 hsk 4
qiàn
to apologize

敲 hsk 4
qiāo
to hit

桥 hsk 4

qiáo

bridge

巧 hsk 4

qiǎo

skillful, clever

且 hsk 4

qiě

moreover

切 hsk 4

qiè

close to, definitely

亲 hsk 4

qīn

parent

琴 hsk 4

qín

musical instrument (in general)

轻 hsk 3

qīng

light (not heavy), soft

清 hsk 3

qīng

clear, pure

情 hsk 2

qíng

feeling

晴 hsk 2

qíng

clear, fine (weather)

请 hsk 1
qǐng
to request

穷 hsk 4
qióng
poor, destitute

秋 hsk 3
qiū
autumn

求 hsk 3
qiú
to seek

球 hsk 2
qiú
ball

区 hsk 4
qū
area, district, region, distinguish

取 hsk 4
qǔ
to take

去 hsk 1
qù
to go

趣 hsk 3
qù
interesting

全 hsk 4
quán
all

泉 hsk 4

quán

spring (small stream)

缺 hsk 4

quē

deficiency

却 hsk 4

què

but

确 hsk 4

què

authentic, firm, real

裙 hsk 3

qún

skirt

然 hsk 2

rán

correct

染 hsk 4

rǎn

to contaminate, catch (a disease), dye

让 hsk 2

ràng

to give way, let somebody do something, yield

扰 hsk 4

rǎo

to disturb

热 hsk 1

rè

heat

人 hsk 1
rén
person

认 hsk 1
rèn
to recognize

任 hsk 4
rèn
to assign

扔 hsk 4
rēng
to throw

仍 hsk 4
réng
still

日 hsk 2
rì
day, sun

容 hsk 3
róng
to hold

肉 hsk 2
ròu
meat

如 hsk 3
rú
in compliance with, like, as

入 hsk 4
rù
to enter

赛 hsk 3

sài

to compete

三 hsk 1

sān

three

伞 hsk 3

sǎn

umbrella

散 hsk 4

sàn

to scatter, let out

扫 hsk 3

sǎo

to sweep

色 hsk 2

sè

color

森 hsk 4

sēn

forest, luxuriant vegetation

沙 hsk 4

shā

granule, powder

山 hsk 3

shān

mountain

衫 hsk 3

shān

garment

伤 hsk 4

shāng

to injure

商 hsk 1

shāng

commerce, merchant, discuss

上 hsk 1

shàng

upon

烧 hsk 3

shāo

to burn

稍 hsk 4

shāo

somewhat

勺 hsk 4

sháo

spoon

少 hsk 1

shǎo

few

绍 hsk 2

shào

to continue

社 hsk 4

shè

society

申 hsk 4

shēn

to extend

身 hsk 2

shēn

body

深 hsk 4

shēn

deep, depth

什 hsk 1

shén

what

甚 hsk 4

shèn

very

生 hsk 1

shēng

to be born

声 hsk 3

shēng

voice

省 hsk 4

shěng

province, to economize, save

剩 hsk 4

shèng

to remain

匙 hsk 4

shi

key

失 hsk 4

shī

to lose

师 hsk 1

shī

teacher

十 hsk 1

shí

ten

时 hsk 1

shí

o'clock, time

识 hsk 1

shí

to know

实 hsk 3

shí

real

拾 hsk 4

shí

to pick up

史 hsk 3

shǐ

history

使 hsk 4

shǐ

to make, use, send on a mission, cause

始 hsk 2

shǐ

to begin

士 hsk 4

shì

scholar, specialist worker

世 hsk 3

shì

life, generation

市 hsk 3

shì

market

示 hsk 4

shì

to show

式 hsk 4

shì

type

事 hsk 2

shì

matter

视 hsk 1

shì

to look at

试 hsk 2

shì

to test

室 hsk 2

shì

room

是 hsk 1

shì

to be

柿 hsk 4

shì

persimmon (fruit)

适 hsk 4
shì
to fit

释 hsk 4
shì
to explain

收 hsk 4
shōu
to receive

手 hsk 2
shǒu
hand

首 hsk 4
shǒu
head

受 hsk 4
shòu
to receive

售 hsk 4
shòu
to sell, carry out (a plan or intrigue)

授 hsk 4
shòu
to teach

瘦 hsk 3
shòu
thin

书 hsk 1
shū
book

叔 hsk 3
shū
uncle

舒 hsk 3
shū
to stretch

输 hsk 4
shū
to lose

熟 hsk 4
shú
familiar, cooked (of food), ripe (of fruit)

暑 hsk 4
shǔ
hot weather

术 hsk 4
shù
skill

束 hsk 3
shù
to bind, control

树 hsk 3
shù
tree

数 hsk 3
shù
number

刷 hsk 3
shuā
to brush

帅 hsk 4

shuài

handsome

双 hsk 3

shuāng

double, pair

谁 hsk 1

shuí

who

水 hsk 1

shuǐ

water

睡 hsk 1

shuì

to sleep

顺 hsk 4

shùn

to obey

说 hsk 1

shuō

to speak

硕 hsk 4

shuò

large

司 hsk 2

sī

to take charge of

思 hsk 2

sī

to think

死 hsk 4

sǐ

to die

四 hsk 1

sì

four

松 hsk 4

sōng

to loose, relax

送 hsk 2

sòng

to deliver

嗽 hsk 4

sòu

cough

诉 hsk 2

sù

to tell

速 hsk 4

sù

fast

塑 hsk 4

sù

to mould, plastic

酸 hsk 4

suān

sour

算 hsk 3

suàn

to regard as

虽 hsk 2
suī
although

随 hsk 4
suí
to follow

岁 hsk 1
suì
classifier for years (of age)

孙 hsk 4
sūn
grandson

所 hsk 2
suǒ
place, part. Introducing a relative clause or passive

他 hsk 1
tā
he, him

它 hsk 2
tā
it, its

她 hsk 1
tā
she, her

台 hsk 4
tái
platform, abbr. for Taiwan

抬 hsk 4
tái
to lift

太 hsk 1

tài

highest

态 hsk 4

tài

attitude

谈 hsk 4

tán

to speak

弹 hsk 4

tán

to play (a string instrument)

汤 hsk 4

tāng

soup

糖 hsk 4

táng

sugar

躺 hsk 4

tǎng

to recline

趟 hsk 4

tàng

classifier for times, round trips or rows

萄 hsk 4

táo

grape

讨 hsk 4

tǎo

to discuss, provoke, send armed forces to suppress

特 hsk 3
tè
special

疼 hsk 3
téng
(it) hurts

梯 hsk 3
tī
ladder

踢 hsk 2
tī
to kick

提 hsk 3
tí
to carry (hanging down from the hand)

题 hsk 2
tí
topic

体 hsk 2
tǐ
body or part of the body, style, form

天 hsk 1
tiān
day

甜 hsk 3
tián
sweet

填 hsk 4
tián
to fill, stuff

条 hsk 2

tiáo

strip; classifier for something long, narrow, thin

跳 hsk 2

tiào

to jump

铁 hsk 3

tiě

iron (metal)

厅 hsk 4

tīng

(reception) hall

听 hsk 1

tīng

to listen

停 hsk 4

tíng

to stop

挺 hsk 4

tǐng

straight

通 hsk 4

tōng

to go through

同 hsk 1

tóng

similar

童 hsk 4

tóng

child, virgin

桶 hsk 4 **tǒng** bucket	头 hsk 3 **tóu** head
突 hsk 3 **tū** to dash, sudden	图 hsk 3 **tú** picture, drawing
推 hsk 4 **tuī** to push	腿 hsk 3 **tuǐ** leg
脱 hsk 4 **tuō** to shed	袜 hsk 4 **wà** sock
外 hsk 2 **wài** outside	完 hsk 2 **wán** to finish

玩 hsk 2
wán
to play, have fun

晚 hsk 2
wǎn
evening

碗 hsk 3
wǎn
bowl

万 hsk 3
wàn
ten thousand

网 hsk 3
wǎng
net

往 hsk 2
wǎng
to go (in a direction)

忘 hsk 3
wàng
to forget

望 hsk 2
wàng
to expect

危 hsk 4
wēi
to endanger

微 hsk 4
wēi
tiny

为 hsk 2

wéi / wèi

to do, because of

围 hsk 4

wéi

to encircle

喂 hsk 1

wéi / wèi

hello (when answering the phone) / v. to feed, raise

卫 hsk 4

wèi

to guard, defend

位 hsk 3

wèi

position

味 hsk 4

wèi

taste

温 hsk 4

wēn

warm, temperature

文 hsk 3

wén

language

闻 hsk 3

wén

news, story

问 hsk 2

wèn

to ask

我 hsk 1

wǒ

I, me, my

污 hsk 4

wū

dirty

无 hsk 4

wú

not to have

五 hsk 1

wǔ

five

午 hsk 1

wǔ

noon

舞 hsk 2

wǔ

to dance

务 hsk 2

wù

business, matter, affair

物 hsk 3

wù

thing, object, creature

误 hsk 4

wù

mistake

吸 hsk 4

xī

to breathe

西 hsk 1 **xī** west	希 hsk 2 **xī** to hope
息 hsk 2 **xī** to breathe, news	悉 hsk 4 **xī** in all cases
惜 hsk 4 **xī** to cherish	习 hsk 1 **xí** to practice
洗 hsk 2 **xǐ** to wash	喜 hsk 1 **xǐ** to be fond of
戏 hsk 3 **xì** trick, play	系 hsk 1 **xì** to connect

细 hsk 4
xì
thin, slender, delicate

下 hsk 1
xià
below

夏 hsk 3
xià
summer

先 hsk 1
xiān
first

鲜 hsk 3
xiān
fresh

咸 hsk 4
xián
salted

险 hsk 4
xiǎn
danger

现 hsk 1
xiàn
to appear

线 hsk 4
xiàn
thread

羡 hsk 4
xiàn
to envy

相 hsk 3 **xiāng** each other	香 hsk 3 **xiāng** fragrant
箱 hsk 3 **xiāng** box	详 hsk 4 **xiáng** detailed
响 hsk 3 **xiǎng** sound, echo	想 hsk 1 **xiǎng** to think
向 hsk 3 **xiàng** towards	象 hsk 4 **xiàng** elephant
像 hsk 3 **xiàng** to resemble	橡 hsk 4 **xiàng** oak

消 hsk 4
xiāo
to disappear

小 hsk 1
xiǎo
small

效 hsk 4
xiào
effect

校 hsk 1
xiào
school

笑 hsk 2
xiào
laugh

些 hsk 1
xiē
some

鞋 hsk 3
xié
shoe

写 hsk 1
xiě
to write

谢 hsk 1
xiè
to thank

心 hsk 3
xīn
heart

辛 hsk 4

xīn

hard, laborious, (of taste) hot or pungent

新 hsk 2

xīn

new

信 hsk 3

xìn

letter, trust

星 hsk 1

xīng

star

醒 hsk 4

xǐng

to wake up, become aware

兴 hsk 1

xìng

feeling or desire to do something

姓 hsk 2

xìng

family name

幸 hsk 4

xìng

fortunate

性 hsk 4

xìng

nature, attribute, sex

熊 hsk 3

xióng

bear

休 hsk 2

xiū

to rest

修 hsk 4

xiū

to decorate

羞 hsk 4

xiū

shy

秀 hsk 4

xiù

elegant, graceful, superior

须 hsk 3

xū

to have to

需 hsk 3

xū

to require

许 hsk 4

xǔ

to allow, praise, perhaps

序 hsk 4

xù

order, sequence

续 hsk 4

xù

to continue, replenish

选 hsk 3

xuǎn

to choose

学 hsk 1
xué
to learn

雪 hsk 2
xuě
snow

呀 hsk 4
ya
(particle equivalent to 啊 after a vowel, expressing surprise or doubt)

压 hsk 4
yā
to press

鸭 hsk 4
yā
duck

牙 hsk 3
yá
tooth

亚 hsk 4
yà
Asia

烟 hsk 4
yān
smoke, cigar, cigarette

严 hsk 4
yán
tight (closely sealed)

言 hsk 4
yán
words

研 hsk 4

yán

to research, grind

盐 hsk 4

yán

salt

颜 hsk 2

yán

color, face, countenance

眼 hsk 2

yǎn

eye

演 hsk 4

yǎn

to act

厌 hsk 4

yàn

to loathe

验 hsk 4

yàn

to examine

扬 hsk 4

yáng

to raise

羊 hsk 2

yáng

sheep

阳 hsk 3

yáng

sun

洋 hsk 4
yáng
vast

养 hsk 4
yǎng
to raise (animals)

样 hsk 1
yàng
manner

邀 hsk 4
yāo
to invite

药 hsk 2
yào
medicine

要 hsk 2
yào
to demand

钥 hsk 4
yào
key

爷 hsk 3
yé
grandpa

也 hsk 2
yě
also

业 hsk 3
yè
line of business

叶 hsk 4
yè
leaf

页 hsk 4
yè
page

一 hsk 1
yī
num. one

衣 hsk 1
yī
to dress

医 hsk 1
yī
medical

宜 hsk 2
yí
proper

姨 hsk 3
yí
mother's sister

疑 hsk 4
yí
to doubt

已 hsk 2
yǐ
already

以 hsk 2
yǐ
to use

椅 hsk 1
yǐ
chair

忆 hsk 4
yì
to recollect

艺 hsk 4
yì
skill

议 hsk 3
yì
to comment on

译 hsk 4
yì
to translate

易 hsk 3
yì
easy

谊 hsk 4
yì
friendship

意 hsk 2
yì
idea

因 hsk 2
yīn
cause

阴 hsk 2
yīn
overcast (weather)

音 hsk 3

yīn

sound

银 hsk 3

yín

silver; relating to money or currency

引 hsk 4

yǐn

to draw (a bow), lead, induce, attract

饮 hsk 3

yǐn

(yin3) to drink

印 hsk 4

yìn

to print, engrave, mark

应 hsk 3

yīng / yìng

to agree / to answer

迎 hsk 3

yíng

to welcome

赢 hsk 4

yíng

to win

影 hsk 1

yǐng

picture

永 hsk 4

yǒng

perpetually, forever

泳 hsk 2

yǒng

swimming

勇 hsk 4

yǒng

brave

用 hsk 3

yòng

to use

优 hsk 4

yōu

excellent

幽 hsk 4

yōu

remote, secluded

尤 hsk 4

yóu

outstanding

由 hsk 4

yóu

from, cause, to follow

邮 hsk 3

yóu

post (office)

油 hsk 4

yóu

oil

游 hsk 2

yóu

to walk

友 hsk 1

yǒu

friend

有 hsk 1

yǒu

to have

又 hsk 3

yòu

also

右 hsk 2

yòu

right (-hand)

于 hsk 3

yú

(indicating time or place) in, on, at

鱼 hsk 2

yú

fish

愉 hsk 4

yú

pleased

与 hsk 4

yǔ / yù

v. give, prep. with, conj. and / v. take part in

羽 hsk 4

yǔ

feather

雨 hsk 1

yǔ

rain

语 hsk 1
yǔ
dialect

育 hsk 3
yù
to educate

预 hsk 4
yù
to advance

遇 hsk 3
yù
to encounter

元 hsk 3
yuán
unit of money (in PRC: Chinese yuan, in USA: dollar, etc)

员 hsk 2
yuán
person engaged in some field of activity

园 hsk 3
yuán
site used for public recreation

原 hsk 4
yuán
former

远 hsk 2
yuǎn
far

院 hsk 1
yuàn
courtyard

愿 hsk 3 **yuàn** to hope	约 hsk 4 **yuē** to make an appointment
月 hsk 1 **yuè** moon, month	阅 hsk 4 **yuè** to inspect
越 hsk 3 **yuè** to exceed	云 hsk 4 **yún** cloud
允 hsk 4 **yǔn** to permit, just	运 hsk 2 **yùn** to move
杂 hsk 4 **zá** mixed	再 hsk 1 **zài** again

在 hsk 1
zài
(located) at

咱 hsk 4
zán
we (speaker + person spoken to)

暂 hsk 4
zàn
of short duration

脏 hsk 4
zāng / zàng
dirty / (anatomy) organ

早 hsk 2
zǎo
early

澡 hsk 3
zǎo
bath

则 hsk 4
zé
conjunction used to express contrast with a previous sentence or clause

择 hsk 3
zé
to select

责 hsk 4
zé
responsibility

怎 hsk 1
zěn
how

增 hsk 4

zēng

to increase

展 hsk 4

zhǎn

to spread out

占 hsk 4

zhàn

to take possession of

站 hsk 2

zhàn

station

张 hsk 3

zhāng

to open up

章 hsk 4

zhāng

chapter

丈 hsk 2

zhàng

husband

招 hsk 4

zhāo

to recruit

着 hsk 2

zháo / zhe

to be troubled with / part. indicating action in progress

找 hsk 2

zhǎo

to try to find

照 hsk 3 **zhào** according to	折 hsk 4 **zhé** a loss
者 hsk 3 **zhě** (after a noun) person involved in ...	这 hsk 1 **zhè** pron. this, these
针 hsk 4 **zhēn** needle	真 hsk 2 **zhēn** really
争 hsk 4 **zhēng** to strive for	整 hsk 4 **zhěng** exactly
正 hsk 2 **zhèng** just (right)	证 hsk 4 **zhèng** to admonish

之 hsk 4

zhī

(possessive part., literary equivalent of 的 de), (used in place of an objective noun or pronoun)

支 hsk 4

zhī

to support

汁 hsk 4

zhī

juice

只 hsk 3

zhī / zhǐ

nm. single / adv. only

知 hsk 2

zhī

to know

直 hsk 3

zhí

straight

值 hsk 4

zhí

value

职 hsk 4

zhí

duty

植 hsk 4

zhí

to grow, set up, plant

止 hsk 4

zhǐ

to stop

址 hsk 4
zhǐ
location

纸 hsk 2
zhǐ
paper

指 hsk 4
zhǐ
finger

至 hsk 4
zhì
to arrive

志 hsk 4
zhì
aspiration, sign

质 hsk 4
zhì
nature, character

中 hsk 1
zhōng
within, middle, abbr. for China

终 hsk 3
zhōng
finish, end

钟 hsk 1
zhōng
time (measure of)

种 hsk 3
zhǒng
seed

众 hsk 4
zhòng
many

重 hsk 3
zhòng
heavy

周 hsk 3
zhōu
week, circumference

洲 hsk 4
zhōu
continent

主 hsk 3
zhǔ
owner

住 hsk 1
zhù
to live

助 hsk 2
zhù
to help

注 hsk 3
zhù
to concentrate, to pour into

祝 hsk 4
zhù
to express good wishes

著 hsk 4
zhù
to make known

专 hsk 4

zhuān

for a particular person, occasion, purpose

转 hsk 4

zhuǎn

to turn

赚 hsk 4

zhuàn

to earn

准 hsk 2

zhǔn

to allow

桌 hsk 1

zhuō

table

子 hsk 1

zi / zǐ

noun suffix / son, child, person

资 hsk 4

zī

resources

仔 hsk 4

zǐ

meticulous

字 hsk 1

zì

letter

自 hsk 3

zì

self

总 hsk 3
zǒng
always

走 hsk 2
zǒu
to walk

租 hsk 1
zū
to hire

足 hsk 2
zú
foot

族 hsk 4
zú
ethnicity, clan

嘴 hsk 3
zuǐ
mouth, beak, spout (of teapot)

最 hsk 2
zuì
most

尊 hsk 4
zūn
senior, venerate

昨 hsk 1
zuó
yesterday

左 hsk 2
zuǒ
left

作 hsk 1

zuò
to do

坐 hsk 1

zuò
to sit

座 hsk 4

zuò
seat

做 hsk 1

zuò
to make

© HSK Academy

Made in United States
North Haven, CT
31 May 2023

37203115R00063